SNAKES

Biggest! Littlest!

by **Sandra Markle**

Photographs by Joe McDonald

Boyds Mills Press

Some snakes are big.

This is a young Reticulated Python
(*Re-TIK-yuh-lay-ted PIE-thawn*).

It's one of the world's biggest
kinds of snakes.

Some Reticulated Pythons are as long
as a city bus.

*The snake on the cover is an Anaconda
(AN-uh-KON-duh).*

*It's another of the world's biggest
kinds of snakes.*

*It's as thick as a man's thigh and weighs
as much as two big men.*

Some snakes are little.

Each of these young Garter Snakes is about as long as an adult's hand.

When they are grown, they are still likely to be shorter than a person's forearm.

Garter Snakes are one of the world's littlest kinds of snakes.

The Blind Snake is even smaller.

An adult is no bigger than a large earthworm.

Some snakes have big parts.

The fangs of a Gaboon Viper *(GAH-boon VY-per)* are about one inch (2.5 centimeters) long .

They are the longest fangs of any kind of snake.

The skin around each fang is a pouch.

The fangs are so long, they have to fold up inside these pouches.

Rattle

**Eastern
Diamondback
Rattlesnake**

Some snakes grow parts that get bigger year by year, like the rattle on this rattlesnake's tail.

When the snake shakes its tail super fast, the rattle makes a noise.

The bigger the rattle, the louder the noise.

How does it help some snakes to be big or little?

How does it help some snakes to have extra big parts?

To find out, you'll need to see how a snake lives.

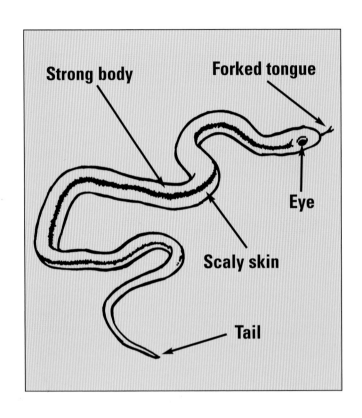

Strong body

Forked tongue

Eye

Scaly skin

Tail

First, all snakes are hunters.

They must catch other animals to eat.

The animals they eat are called the snakes' *prey*.

So snakes have bodies built for hunting.

Snakes have no legs.

That lets them hide under rocks and slip through narrow spaces.

And it lets some snakes easily wrap around and hold onto prey.

A snake doesn't stab prey with its forked tongue.

Keep reading this book to find out how the snake's special tongue helps it hunt.

The Cantil (KAN-til) has a colorful tail with a special use.

It's bait.

The snake makes its tail wiggle like a worm.

When lizards and frogs try to catch the "worm," the snake catches them.

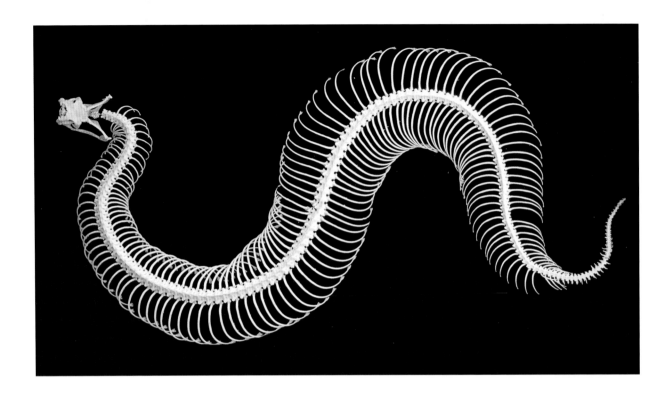

Snakes can crawl, swim, and climb to hunt.

That's because they have lots of bones to let their bodies bend easily.

And they have strong muscles to move their bones.

So snakes can loop side-to-side or push and pull themselves forward.

How many backbones do you see?

People have only 33, but snakes can have hundreds.

Snakes' bodies are covered with scales.

These are spots of thick fingernail-like material on stretchy skin.

Scales keep snakes from being hurt as they crawl over sharp rocks, through thorny brush, and up rough tree bark.

Python

The scales on a snake's back are small and overlap like roof shingles.

These act like armor to shield the snake.

The scales are also colored.

The Green Bush Viper's scales help it blend in and sneak up on prey.

The scales on a snake's belly are big and flat.

These act like tire tread to dig in and pull the snake along.

This Green Bush Viper's big belly scales make it a great tree climber.

Snakes have one big, clear scale over each eye.

These cover the eyes like goggles.

So the Horned Desert Viper can hide in the sand and not get grit in its eyes while it watches for prey.

No one is sure why this snake has horns.

Some scientists think the horns may help keep things from dropping onto the snake's eyes.

But snakes do not have keen eyesight.

A snake uses its tongue to help it find prey.

Flicking out its tongue, the Copperhead picks up tiny bits of scent matter in the air.

When it pulls its tongue back into its mouth, the snake "smells" if prey is nearby.

The forked shape lets the snake judge whether the scent is strongest on the right or left.

That helps the snake find its prey, even in the dark.

Some snakes catch and kill prey by looping around it.

This big African Rock Python caught a gazelle, which is about as big as a white-tail deer.

Then the snake squeezed to make its kill.

The Python's big size lets it catch and kill prey that are too big for most other snakes to hunt.

Some snakes overpower prey and swallow it alive.

That's how the little Garter Snake gets a meal.

But it kills small prey like this frog.

Such little prey isn't enough food for bigger snakes to bother with.

So Garter Snakes can live around bigger snakes and not compete for meals.

Big or little, all snakes swallow their prey whole!

Now you can see the stretchy skin between the snake's scales.

All of a snake's teeth are sharp.

They are not the right shape for chewing.

So snakes have mouths built to open wide enough to swallow a whole meal all at once.

A snake's upper and lower jaws are hooked together by stretchy bands and muscles.

A snake's lower jawbone is made up of two pieces. (A person's is made of just one.)

These two pieces are also hooked together by stretchy bands.

This Egg-eating Snake can open its mouth even wider than most snakes can.

So it can swallow bigger eggs than other snakes that eat bird's eggs.

For this snake, it's good to have a really big mouth!

The Egg-eating Snake does not eat the egg's shell, though.

The snake's muscles push the egg against its backbones until the shell cracks.

Then the snake swallows the gooey yolk and white and throws up the shell.

Snakes can even swallow while hanging upside down.

That's because all of a snake's teeth are aimed backwards, toward its throat.

To swallow, the snake moves first one half of its upper and lower jaws and then the other half.

That pulls the snake's body over its food.

Blanding's Tree Snake

Eating gives a snake the food energy it needs to grow bigger.

But a snake's tough outer skin is like a snug body suit.

So when the snake grows, it sheds its skin.

It peels off in one piece—usually inside-out.

That leaves the slightly bigger snake with a new, bigger body suit of skin.

**Eastern
Diamondback
Rattlesnake**

A rattlesnake's rattle also grows bigger each time it sheds.

And that's about four times a year.

A baby rattlesnake is born with a button on its tail.

It doesn't make any noise.

But each time the snake sheds, one piece of skin sticks to its tail button.

When the snake shakes its tail fast, these bump together and make a noise. *Buzzzzzzz!*

Western Diamondback Rattlesnake

After the snake's rattle gets really long, the oldest bits at the tip break off.

The rattlesnake uses its rattle to stay safe.

When an animal comes close, the rattlesnake shakes its tail.

That means, "Go away!"

Most animals obey.

That's because a rattlesnake is armed with special teeth called fangs.

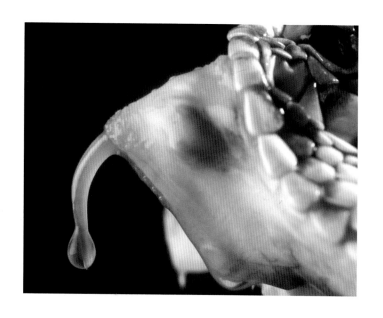

These are the fangs of an Eastern Diamondback Rattlesnake.

What's dripping out is a kind of poison called venom (*VEN-um*).

The Eastern Diamondback Rattlesnake can grow longer than a tall basketball player.

It is the biggest kind of venomous (*VEN-um-us*) snake in the United States.

Besides biting to defend itself, this snake bites to kill its prey.

A rattlesnake's fangs drop out and are replaced by new ones about every two months.

Timber Rattlesnake

Venom also breaks down the prey's tissues.

So the snake's meal is starting to digest even before it's swallowed.

But the rattlesnake's venom does not kill right away.

To avoid a fight, the rattlesnake lets its prey escape.

Next, the snake follows its prey until the venom does its job.

Then the rattlesnake swallows its meal.

Not all rattlesnakes are big.

The Dusky Pygmy Rattlesnake is only about as long as a shoebox.

Being small helps this snake hide and strike any prey that comes close.

But the snake's venom only packs a little punch.

So the Dusky Pygmy Rattlesnake hunts little prey, like lizards, frogs, and mice.

Sometimes, big and little kinds of rattlesnakes share the same hunting area.

But being different sizes means they're not likely to hunt the same prey.

Remember the Gaboon Viper's fangs?

These long teeth let the snake inject its venom deep into its prey.

And that helps the snake kill fast.

So the Gaboon Viper can safely hold on and not use up energy tracking down its prey.

The King Cobra (*KOH-bruh*) is longer than the average car.

Its head is as big as a man's hand.

This snake is one of the world's biggest kinds of venomous snakes.

But it has little fangs.

The tube in the snake's mouth is its windpipe.

When swallowing its prey, a snake pushes its windpipe forward.

Then it can breathe while its throat is blocked.

The King Cobra makes up for its little fangs by injecting very powerful venom.

The King Cobra mainly hunts other big snakes.

So injecting powerful venom lets this snake hunt prey that would be too dangerous for most snakes.

A King Cobra's bite could kill a full-grown elephant!

Look at these hatching baby pythons.

They will grow up to be BIG snakes.

Growing up for a baby snake is all about becoming as big or as little as it was meant to be.

A snake's size is its very life.

Some are big.

Some are little.

Others have extra-big parts.

That is how each different kind of snake has adapted to live in its own special part of the world.

Where in the world do these snakes live?

Check the map to see where they were photographed.

THAILAND
King Cobra
(18 feet/5.4 meters)
Reticulated Python
(33 feet/10 meters)

KENYA
African Rock Python
(20 feet/6 meters)

MEXICO
Cantil
(3 feet/0.9 meters)

UNITED STATES
Blind Snake
(8 inches/20 centimeters)
Copperhead
(3 feet/0.9 meters)
Dusky Pygmy Rattlesnake
(22 inches/55 centimeters)
Eastern Diamondback Rattlesnake
(8 feet/2.4 meters)

Garter Snake
(30 inches/75 centimeters)
Timber Rattlesnake
(3.5 feet/1 meter)
Western Diamondback Rattlesnake
(7 feet/2.1 meters)

BRAZIL
Anaconda
(18 feet/5.4 meters)

NAMIBIA
Horned Desert Viper
(29 inches/75 centimeters)

TANZANIA
Blanding's Tree Snake
(7 feet/2.1 meters)
Egg-eating Snake
(30 inches/75 centimeters)
Gaboon Viper
(6.5 feet/2 meters)
Green Bush Viper
(24 inches/60 centimeters)

With love for Jacob and Jordan Moore and their grandparents, Gail and Wayne Rissman

—S. M.

Snake Words You Learned:

Bones: The hard parts that form a supporting framework for the snake's body.

Fangs: A pair of sharp teeth used to inject venom.

Muscles: Body parts that move the snake's bones by pulling on them.

Prey: An animal the snake catches to eat.

Scale: A place where skin is thicker for extra protection. Together the scales form an outer layer covering the snake's body.

Shed: To remove old skin as the snake's body grows bigger.

Venom: Liquid poison that flows out of the fangs.

Surprising Facts About Snakes

*A big snake, like a Reticulated Python, does not grow more bones as it gets longer. Its bones just get bigger.

* Snakes help people by eating hundreds of mice and rats that would otherwise eat food crops.

*Snakes cannot produce body heat. They warm up by basking in the sun and cool off by moving into the shade.

Photo Credits: p. 2 Clyde Peeling, p. 14 Fritz Polking, pp. 3(bottom), 17-18 Dave Northcott/Nature Lens, all others by Joe McDonald

Acknowledgment: The author would like to thank Dr. Harry W. Greene, curator of herpetology at Cornell University and a noted expert on the biology and natural history of vertebrates, especially snakes. And a special thank you to Skip Jeffery for his help and support.

Note to Parents and Teachers: The books in the BIGGEST! LITTLEST! series encourage children to explore their world. Young readers are encouraged to wonder. Then kids are guided to discover how animals depend on their special body features to be successful in their particular environment.

"Each plant or animal has different structures that serve different functions in growth, survival, and reproduction. An organism's patterns of behavior are related to the nature of that organism's environment, the availability of food, and the physical characteristics of the environment." National Science Education Standards as identified by the National Academy of Sciences.

Back Cover: Copperhead

Text copyright © 2005 by Sandra Markle
Photographs copyright © 2005 by Joe McDonald
All rights reserved

Published by Boyds Mills Press, Inc.
A Highlights Company
815 Church Street
Honesdale, Pennsylvania 18431
Printed in China

2004014576
First edition, 2005
The text of this book
is set in 13-point Minion.
Visit our Web site at
www.boydsmillspress.com

10 9 8 7 6 5 4 3 2 1

Library of Congress Cataloging-in-Publication Data

Markle, Sandra.
  Snakes : biggest! littlest! / by Sandra Markle ; with photographs by Joe McDonald.— 1st ed.
    p. cm.
  ISBN 1-59078-189-9 (alk. paper)
  1. Snakes—Juvenile literature. I. Title.

QL666.O6M2573 2004
597.96--dc22